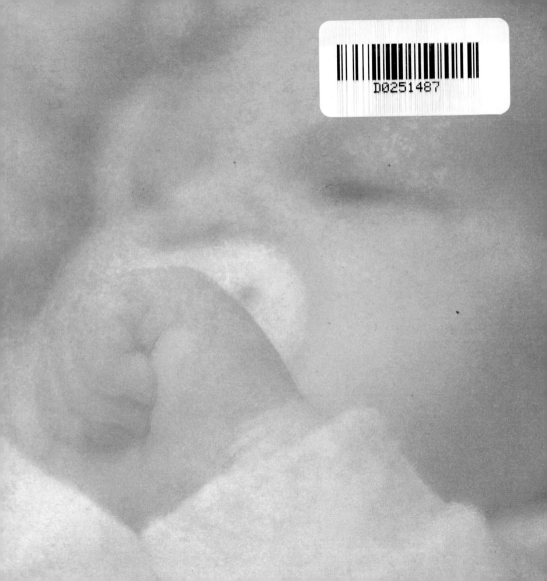

presented to

Robert David Bokenfohr

by

Uncle Dale and Auntie Lynn

on this date

December 5, 1999

BLESS THIS CHILD

GLORIA GAITHER

COUNTRYMAN

FOREWORD

When a baby is born, there is, perhaps, a little window of time when God has everybody's attention. It is important, then, for us all to stop things down and gather to consider what is going on here. All through the Bible, God forbids us to usurp His position by "playing God," but there is one exception. He has made it possible for two human beings to come together in love, to be joined as one flesh and, at that moment, to become co-creators with God of an eternal soul. No wonder such strict religious laws govern our sexual behavior and permit intercourse only in the confines of a faithful marriage union. Something so eternal must be considered sacred and protected against desecration.

But whether human beings have played by the rules or not, there is something holy about a baby. Birth is one of the most sacred passages human beings can experience. So sacred that Jesus Himself used it as a metaphor for the experience of coming to know God—the birth of our spirits—the "second birth."

No baby should come into this world without someone making a moment. This entrance is sacred. All of us who accept the responsibility for handling this new creation should give our blessing to this child, so full of potential. And we should sanctify ourselves as we commit long-term to this new, eternal soul entrusted to our care.

God bless us all!

Gloria Gaither

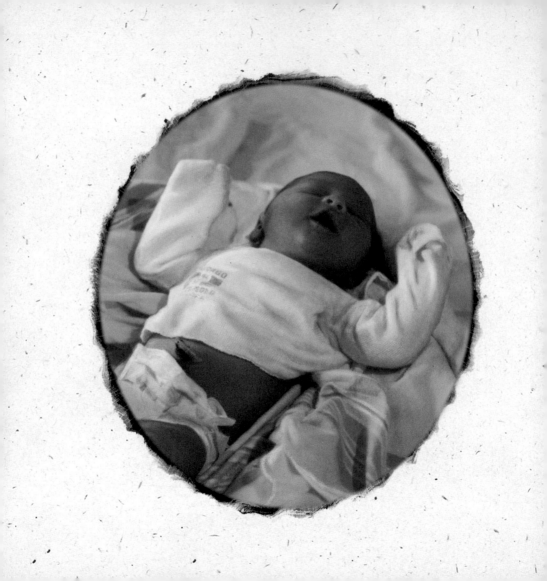

Bless this child.

Bless the parents whose love

conceived this small, new being.

Bless the womb that

nurtured and protected.

Bless the home that made

preparations.

Bless the patience that waited.
Bless the hope that believed what
could not be seen.
Bless the faith that acted on the hope
in waiting.

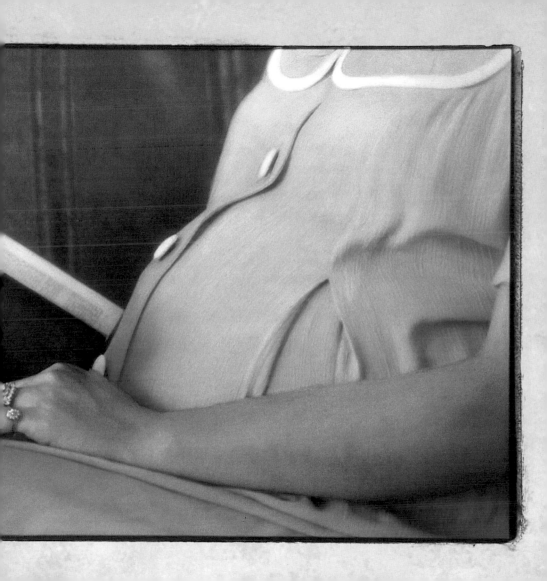

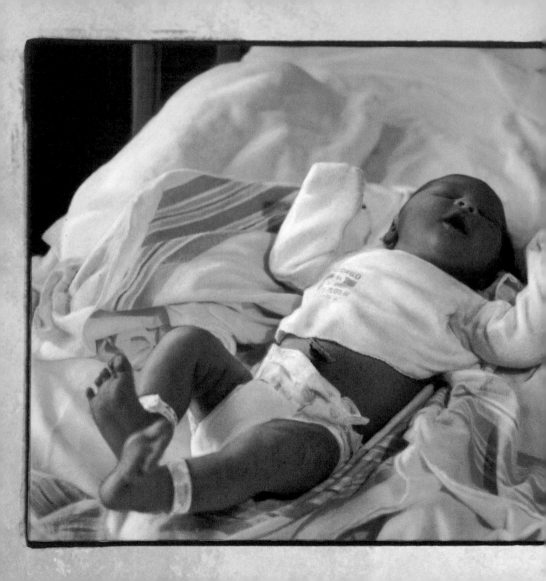

We bless you, new child!
Like the resurrected Christ,
you burst from the confines
that cannot hold your
blossoming life!

Into the morning, fresh with

dew you come.

The dawn fills your lungs

with a triumphant cry,

"Life wins!

Life wins!

I am!"

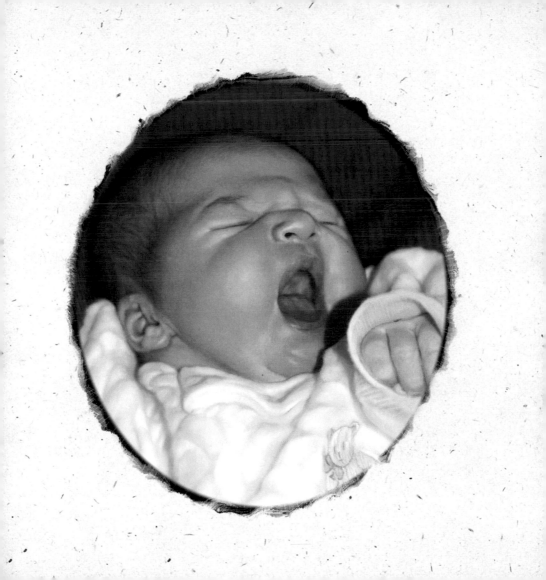

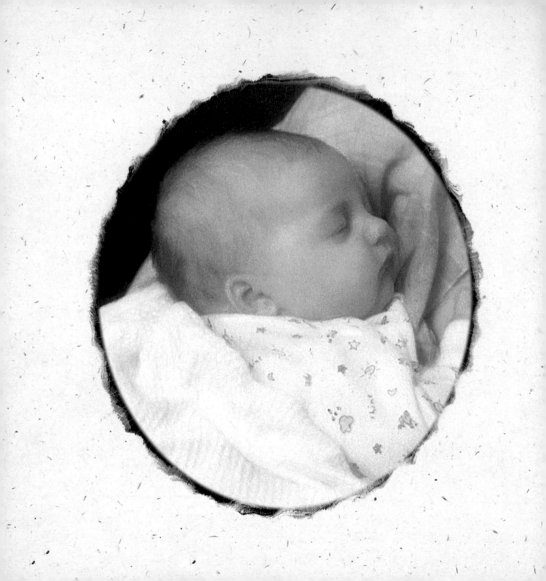

We are amazed at you.

Your whole being throbs with life,

every sinew vibrating,

every compact ounce of you,

pulsating with raw

and virgin energy.

So small you are, yet so powerful!

We are in awe of you.

We cannot take our eyes from you.

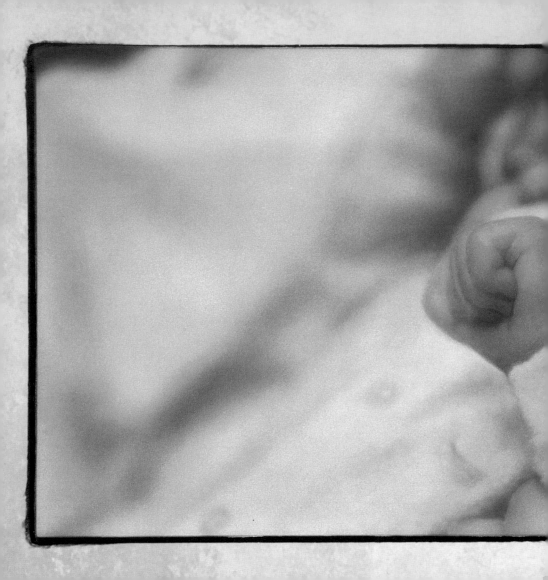

You are a burning bush.

You are a trembling Sinai.

You are a new star in the east.

You are a blinding light on

Damascus.

We kick off our shoes

to gaze at you.

There is something holy

going on here,

and we stare in amazement,

straining to comprehend

the message

carved by the finger

of God

on this freshly

hewn tablet.

Though our senses have been dulled by
too many days

in the too-much-with-us world . . .

we are suddenly aware

that here is reality.

There is something eternal breaking through into this moment.

The lenses of our eyes seem to sharpen their focus.

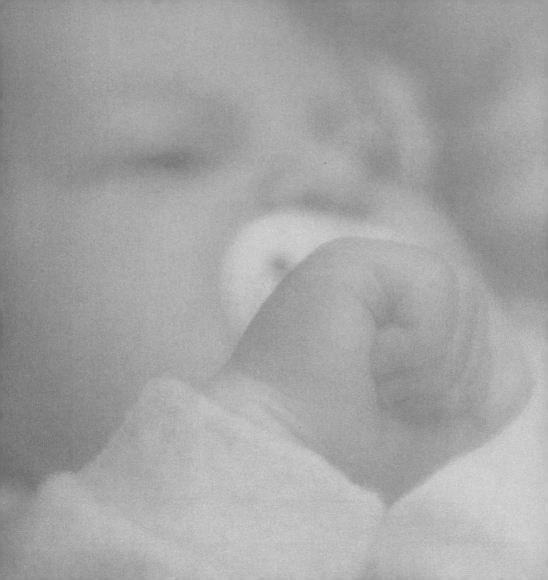

Our hearing becomes acute—

fresh nerve endings seem to

work their way

to the tips of our fingers.

We stroke your velvet skin

still powdered with the dust of

"somewhere else,"

still "trailing clouds of Glory."

W hat mysteries you hold!

What revelations of the Mighty One

  who shaped you in your

  mother's womb,

    who knew you from conception

    and planned each

    moment of your life.

He has known you;

have you known Him who

held you in His hand?

Known Him purely

without the limits

of earth?

What will you teach us,

you so lately come from God?

We would make a sacrament
of your delivery.
We would build a sanctuary here.
We would purify ourselves to
hold you.

We would seek the wisdom of
God to teach you,

for we are not worthy.

We drink the wine of communion

that we may

refresh our communion with

the One who sent you here.

We must know Him and
walk in His paths
if we are to lead you,
for to know that you will
follow in our footsteps is a
fearsome, awesome thing.

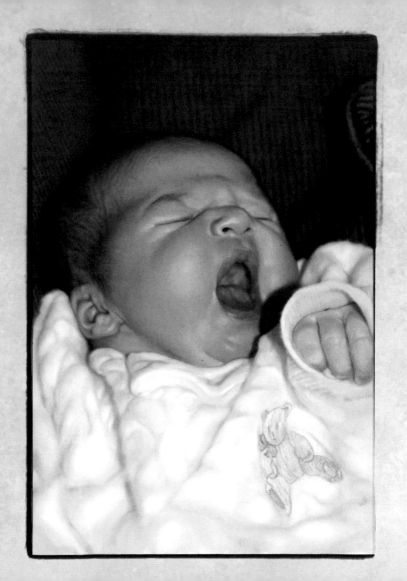

Bless this child.

Bless this tiny mouth and fill it with
your praises.

Bless these small hands.
May they ever reach to touch the
face of God.
May they reach to heal and serve
a broken world.

Bless this eager, hungry mind.
Protect it from the ugly, the

perverse, the cruel.

Fill it with wonder . . .

and with questions that seek

to know the truth.

May this mind find answers that

cure diseases and ease pain,

seek solutions that bring peace

and reconciliation,

make discoveries that

build bridges of

understanding

and bring hope where there has

been suspicion

and despair.

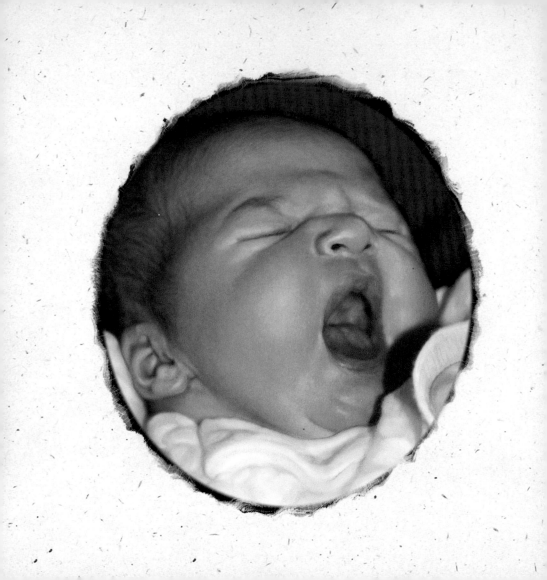

Bless this mouth.

May it learn to speak words
that are helpful, encouraging,
and right.

May these butterfly lips kiss
away injury,

savor the wholesome,

and declare their Maker's

praise.

Bless these feet.

May they run from evil,

pursue justice,

walk in the paths of peace

and leap for joy at

the gift of each new day.

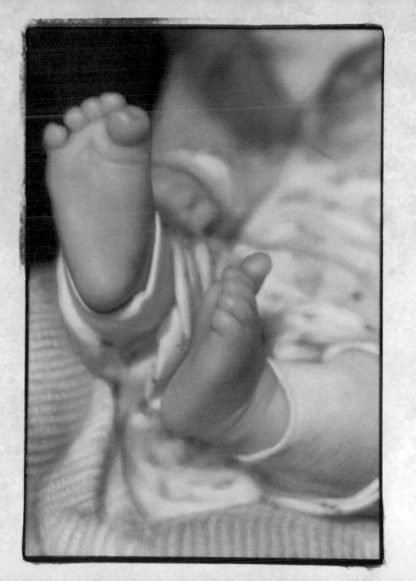

We who touch this tender bud now pledge ourselves in solemn vow

to nurture this child with tenderness—

to teach this child by word and example—

to encourage this child along the paths of upright living.

We commit our energies and resources to provide for the needs of this child's body, mind, and soul,

to defend against forces, seen and unseen,

that would destroy this child's potential

or break this tender spirit by harsh criticism or ugly attitudes.

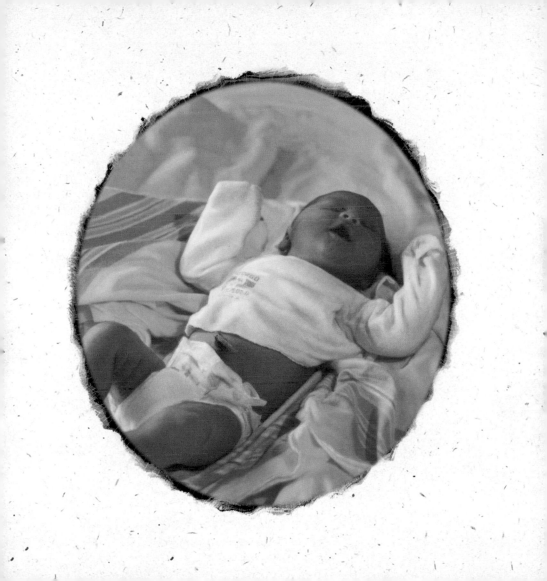

We will protect and encourage the uniqueness that will take this child into uncharted territory.

Even when we may not understand where God is leading, we will help this child follow the wooing of God's heart.

W

e will be there.

When this child is little and

cute, we will be there.

When this child is boisterous

and obnoxious,

we will be there.

When this child is silent,

noncommunicative,

and withdrawn,

we will be there.

When this child is aggressive

and rebellious

and challenges everything we've

ever tried to teach,

we will be there.

When this child is mature,

independent, and efficient,

we will still be there.

We who now gather to

adore this infant

    pledge ourselves to the

    total task

        of loving, nurturing,

        and shaping

        this child.

And when our job is done,

by God's grace, we will

relinquish control

and embrace the joy

of being

this child's most

trusted friends.

Bless you, new child!

BLESSED CHILD!

Baby's full name _____

Date of Birth _____

Place of Birth _____

Height _____

Weight _____

Father's Name _____

Mother's Name _____

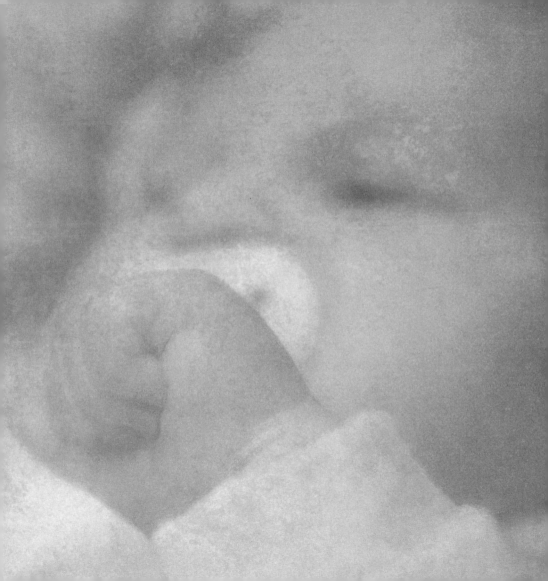